AF422069

COMPLETE OR *Complete*

MAXIMIZING YOUR **SPIRITUAL CALLING** IN THE **MARKETPLACE**

ALEXANDER O. EMOGHENE

Copyright © 2022 Alexander O. Emoghene.

ISBN: 978-94-6437-482-7

All rights reserved. No part of this book may be reproduced, stored, or transmitted by any means—whether auditory, graphic, mechanical, or electronic—without written permission of both publisher and author, except in the case of brief excerpts used in critical articles and reviews. Unauthorized reproduction of any part of this work is illegal and is punishable by law.

Introduction

Maximizing your spiritual
calling in the marketplace

That is the purpose of this book, and I hope to present an option that many may consider implementing in their decision-making, growth plans, and strategies for influence in the future. I hope to help you stand with faith in the marketplace representing the kingdom of God with proven signs following.

This book is all about a change of mind and perspectives, taking you into a different attitude in doing business. It provides essential interpretations on how to avoid or refuse to take on a competitive spirit. Instead, the spirit of completion.

God's command to Adam was to replenish the earth. In other words, to complete it and not fall into a competitive environment.

Contents

A DEFINITION OF THE MARKETPLACE

The marketplace in the scripture refers to those individuals in the business world. Besides this general understanding of the marketplace, there are individuals who do not run a business but are homemakers or are in an employment capacity. They are also vital actors in the marketplace.

A marketplace is a place where critical decisions affect people's lives. The marketplace is also a structure that produces any given society's culture. In the scripture, God reveals the marketplace as a powerful place that needs the right individuals to take on the helms.

Proverbs 29:2...When the godly are in authority, the people rejoice. But when the wicked are in power, they groan. (NLT)

For the sake of this study, I am referring to godly people and how imperative it is for them to come into influential positions at all levels of any society so that they will see humans of any kind flourishing. Individuals with a high sense of righteousness are needful to drive home God's mind and will into the heart of the culture. This E-book will highlight the particularly important elements for the people of the Kingdom of God to step up and accept their place in bringing righteousness in the marketplace.

Additionally, this E-book will deal with crucial subjects that will help you as a believer come to terms with accepting your divine calling by the awareness of your role in the marketplace.

In this edition, I intend to help you maximize your gift as a marketplace believer.

THE CONCEPT OF COSMOS

John 3:16 "For God so loved the world that He gave His only begotten Son, that whoever believes in Him should not perish but have everlasting life."

In this text, Jesus dealt with the aspect of redemption as the chief reason for His work. In this verse, we learned why Jesus Christ came to the earth. His defense highlighted the Love of God concerning the planet.

In conventional bible teaching, the above text usually refers to people and the salvation of souls, which in essence it is, but when we look from the vantage point of the marketplace, aligned with God's holistic plan for redemption. Now all of a sudden a whole different motivation energizes us.

John 3:16, from the marketplace perspective, delivers so many benefits to the kingdom entrepreneur. You will find the secret to the passion of Christ and the heartbeat of the Father concerning his creation. You feel His Love for His creation, and his unending Love for humanity and all this Love expressed in this one verse.

\# So, let us unpack it—The object of God's Love in the world, and in the scripture. There are two words that can be used interchangeably. The first word is earth, and the second is world. In studies, the usage of the earth describes our physical dirt, dust or sand, and our natural world.

So, whenever you see a text that says, for example in Psalms 24:1, "for the earth is the Lord's and the fullness thereof," it describes the physical earth and claims that this physical earth is God's property. The claim is that the earth is the Lord's, and all its fullness belongs to God.

In essence, they are referring to the heavens and the earth. And all its components, all the riches that come with it, such as the mineral reserves. The gold, silver, diamonds, seas creatures like all variety fish and sea life, and everything that humanity needs to flourish in this world. These are what nations built their entire economies on today.

But on the other hand, when the scripture uses the word world, it refers to the complex organisation and the unseen systems and laws that makes the earth function properly. This term is called the cosmos.

\# Cosmos points to both spiritual and natural laws and systems. It speaks about how they ensure humanity lives in harmony with each other and the environment. And God being the supreme caretaker of both the earth and the cosmos.

When God created the earth in Genesis chapter one and chapter two, we find that it is written in the scripture that he finished his creation in seven days. I recognize how unique and vital it is to have Genesis chapters one and two in the Bible. It's remarkable that you'll find no point of disorder, chaos, sin, and the like.

If the book of the Bible did not contain both chapters, we would never have come to understand the Love of God for humanity; nor would we have a reference point to want perfection or excellence truly is. So, Genesis chapter one and two shows us how God's system operates and that when God's system and order are in place, it will only amount to human flourishing and growth together and with God.

"And God being the supreme caretaker of both the earth and the cosmos."

So, let's bring together the point of John 3:16 as a motivation of the revelation of perfection revealed in Genesis one and two. It is safe to deduce from "for God so loved the world that he sent his only begotten son," as saying; "God so love order! Therefore, His Love for order and the potential beauty order can create motivated Him to send His only begotten Son.

It is so vital to address why the aforementioned discussion is notable. In the garden of Eden story, God created total order before He made Adam. Therefore, establishing that order or cosmos is man's natural habitat. When sin came, it disrupted this environment of order that God initiated with the redemption project.

On the surface, this looks counterintuitive; one may ask, why not restore Adam (mankind) first, before his environment? He loves human beings, but His Love for orderliness is more significant than the restoration of humanity. So, bringing back the cosmos and all that it takes to claim it means humans can flourish in their original habitat. They can live in harmony and influence to succeed in a complete order spiritually, financially, and materially.

Kingdom entrepreneurship in the marketplace will determine whether the quest to redeem the cosmos/order is plausible because the marketplace is an excellent determinant of how our cosmos works.

A marketplace dominated by unrighteousness will gravitate toward the lowest cravings that destroy the fabric of societies in the world as we see it today. When the marketplace becomes corrupted and consumed by greed and self-centeredness, you will find the disorder as the order of the day.

So, John 3:16 is an announcement that God loves the order and the systems he put in place, and by the coming of Jesus Christ and his redemptive work on the cross, He is to restore the cosmos, which is the best environment for humans to live, rule and reign on the earth. This redemptive work is not over yet; it is an ongoing project until the end comes.

#BRINGING THE CHANGE

Mark 16:15…And he said unto them, go ye into all the world, and preach the gospel to every creature.

Let us now focus on how best to elaborate on this ongoing redemption project and where it finds the most expression.

Firstly, this text is where we derive the context of the great commission. This text will deliver to

the hands of any kingdom businessperson the best vantage point for your assignment and how you can get involved in God's project of redemption. Jesus charges His Apostle to go in all the world and preach the gospel. From our earlier word exposition. I believe the context of John 3:16 receives a new light.

Jesus commissioned the Apostles to go into all the cosmos to bring or restore His created order of operation which by now is hijacked by "satan and his cohorts." As you know, this will not just take the preaching of the word, but a strong entrepreneurial spirit, strategic leadership, growing influence, and affluence.

\# Secondly, to preach means to announce. In many ways, to announce means making an event public that has already taken place. It is like reporting a car incident or any other memorable event worth reporting. The event is the good news or "gospel" for this write-up.

One may ask, what is "the good news?"

\# Well, Jesus's death, burial, and resurrection (1Corinthians 15:1-4) have kick-started all rights to get involved in God's redemption project. Right off the bat, the angels celebrated this great start when Jesus Christ was born by declaring God's prosperity and goodwill toward all men. (Luke 2:14... "Glory to God in the highest, and on earth peace, goodwill toward men!")

#BEST PRACTICE IN PREACHING

"Responsible preaching must focus on strategies to convey God's Kingdom into the market space."

When we think of preaching, traditionally, we mostly think of the public declaration of the preaching from the pulpit on a Sunday morning. The context in which the Apostle heard Jesus's charge must have been one of the greatest motivations. Not only to preach from a pulpit but to change their world as they know it.

They saw a cosmos that needed restoration from the decay of disorder, sin, and death. They did not create a pulpit. Instead,

they went as one man into all the systems in their day to announce the kingdom of God and God's plan to redeem all systems back to God's original intent for humanity.

Preaching from a pulpit is significant, and I am a great lover and advocate for gathering the saints together. (Hebrews 10:25) However, responsible preaching must focus on strategies to convey God's Kingdom into the market space. Preaching is the declaration of words and the exercise of kingdom entrepreneurial spirit in the marketplace.

After the verse where Jesus commanded, we should go into all the world and preach the gospel to all creature, it is followed by verse 16, which states,

"He who believes and is baptized will be saved; but he who does not believe will be condemned."

So, the essence of preaching is to change lives; it alleviates human distress and suffering. The gospel improves the lives of individuals when it is accepted. It is to bring the Kingdom of God to the human experience. Hence, a focus on the pulpit ministry may not be sufficient to complete this project.

The other side of preaching, which I call the best practice in preaching, is where we can preach the gospel with our lives as examples of God's grace, wherever we can. And the most important arena for the preaching gospel is reflected in daily Christian lives in the marketplace; massive change can occur, one that can shift the entire culture of a whole region to turn into doing business God ways.

So, for the sake of avoiding repetition, I will define the marketplace again by its implication. Wherever you find yourself operational as a Christian, apart from the gathering of the believers, it is termed the marketplace.

Early Christians influenced their world by their intentional daily living. They were effective because they found opportunities to practically influence culture by structuring their family, friends, and societal living; the engaging and applying kingdom principle at every level of society.

They prioritized their stake in the marketplace as they became more familiarized with what goes on in the world (cosmos), and at the same time they look for ways to establish God's plans. This awareness gave access to early believers to engage in societal issues to bring about kingdom solutions.

Paul recounts the success of the gospel and the fruit of the preaching of the gospel is. Colossians 1:5-6...For the hope, which is laid up for you in heaven, whereof ye heard before in the word of the truth of the gospel; which is come unto you, as it is in all the world; and bringeth forth fruit, as it doth also in you, since the day ye heard of it, and knew the grace of God in truth.

If you sense that you have a call to be in the marketplace instead of the pulpit ministry, you must realize how vital your role is in God's completion plans of redemption. It holds an exceptional place in the heart of God.

#FISHER OF MEN

The great commission to go into the world cannot advance without the culture of heaven influencing the marketplace. That is where the fishing needs to be more active.

Jesus told Peter, "I will make you a fisher of men." In the natural men do not live in water: but, by using this metaphor, by using the symbol of water, Jesus describes the inhabitable marketplace environment that stifles the masses. Jesus showed us the disorder in the marketplace that the masses are drowning to make ends meet.

The sea represents a system riddled with corruption, unforgiving, and competitiveness. These are economic environments that are inhabitable for humans to thrive. God created humans to trust, to share, and to love. We are species that are here to complete each other.

But after the fall of mankind, as it became then and sad to say today, the masses are here in our days, drowning in the world system. This marketplace environment is in operation in the hands of individuals ignorantly under the influence of satan's desires and his cohorts to bring misfortune, pain, stress, loss of identity, greed, the break-up of the homes, and all the ails of society.

"In this complex environment, God wants his people to go and unleash His glory in the marketplace to save lives." People lose their souls in the grind because they "got to do what they got to do." The marketplace saint calling is valuable, and God wants to use His son and daughter as it were to save people from these grave conditions. By giving His children better and unique concepts, ideas, and vision for a brighter future.

In this excellent way of thinking and heavenly perspective, the marketplace will function in a way where all will prosper.

That is why the enemy not only discourages the spiritual side of life but also spends a significant amount of resources to influence the marketplace to avoid any trace of God. As 've mentioned initially, the marketplace is the secret tool deployed correctly by any camp. (The camp of satan or the camp of God's kingdom).

Therefore, the contention we see between the forces of the darkness and the light, exists at all levels. The cosmos can be operated so that it conditions itself for prosperity to all, or it brings poverty, corruption, and greed, depending on who is in the helms of authority. (Proverbs 29:2)

God wants to take it over by bringing his people to the commercial centres of nations where his principles can find expression, so that the norm of hope and prosperity can begin again. As a kingdom businessperson, you can start to feel how relevant your role is in God.

When kingdom businesspeople realize this, they start to feel the enormous pressure and questions, like how do I compete with the big players in my industry? Where is the resource coming from? How can I make a difference? Is it possible to make a difference?

These questions, although legitimate, can stand in the progression of your God-given assignment. So, this book is all about a change of mind and perspectives. It takes you into a different attitude in doing business; it will show you not to take on that competitive spirit but the spirit of completion.

God's command to Adam was to replenish the earth. In other words, to complete it and not fall into a competitive environment.

How best can you maximize your gifting and serve God's purpose of completion through the marketplace? It is the true question. Well, I've devised a helpful and practical precept "to complete." Let us examine these suggestions in the following chapter.

COMPLETE VS COMPETE

As referred to in the previous chapter, the great commission also convey that God wants to use the marketplace ministers to forward His agenda of redemption.

Compete or Complete may sound alike, but they are miles apart in nature, result, and impact to humanity as it relates to the marketplace. Let us start with some definitions which I intentionally went for their (competition and completion) verb entry from webster dictionary.

\# Compete means striving consciously or unconsciously for an objective, (such as position, profit, or a prize) being in a state of rivalry. This definition comes to life when you consider the synonyms attached to this word, such as battle, contend, face-off, fight, race, rival, vie.

\# Complete means to bring to an end, especially into a perfected state, and the second verb entry goes further to define it, to make whole or perfect and for the sake of emphasis, let's throw in the third verb entry; is to carry out (a forward pass) successfully.

Let us first consider the implication of competition or the impact on an individual operating in a competitive spirit or a competitive environment.

#CULTURE OF COMPETITION

Compete is the primary motivation in the marketplace today as we know it. The cut-throat world of stepping over others gets encouraged as the only way to the top.

There is much pressure to perform in a competitive, driven system. To increase profit and position at all costs, many will go into all sorts of inconsistencies, with pricing, shady contracts, "progressive" accounting, to mention a few. The world is suffering right now under this unsustainable system. It is increasingly becoming toxic and counterproductive.

"This spirit of competition drives the pain we all are experiencing."

There is a greater tendency for unethical practices in this competitive space through this unhealthy motivation to win over an opponent at all costs. Competitions feed the passion to battle against one's opponent, rival, and contend with them; this climate takes pre-eminence over best practices and the long-term progression of our communities.

The culture of competition can be very alluring to a kingdom businessperson. It seems you are in the middle of the culture, which forces you to reconsider your norms and values daily; if not, you cannot grasp how to prosper. That is because your spirit can longer cooperate with such toxicity. Many good businesspeople soon become frustrated and give in to the pressure of becoming just like the system they abhor.

You will be confronted with this pressure cooker environment as it were in your daily experiences. The probability of whether to compete is probably the most spiritual challenge that will greet you in the marketplace.

If you choose to accept your marketplace assignment, then the chances that you will be as Joseph in the Bible will be exceptionally high. It comes with this space; it lures one to drop aside righteousness, or rather to see ethical dealings in the marketspace as old-fashioned, needing much modification.

In some cases, because of the nature of this temptation, some well-meaning Christians adapt to unethical and ungodly principles and brush it off as what must be done and beg for God's grace at a later stage.

Their excuse is "at least everyone does it, even some Christians I know do it, what is the big deal; and oh, by the way, what is so special about me?"

Due to this ignorance, many are unaware of how easy it is for a spiritual portal to be opened, which gives the enemy access into their business, causing all kinds of havoc and pain. By such ignorance the enemy can reign in your business. Not many bankruptcies occur because of market conditions or bad planning, all these may have their place, but there is also a spiritual side to sustaining a business when one functions in the favour and success with God.

> \# Uzziah sought God during the days of Zechariah, who taught him to fear God. And as long as the king sought guidance from the LORD, God gave him success. (2 Chronicle 26:5)

The competition module will not produce the desired kingdom results for you as a businessperson, especially when you want to flow in favour of the Lord. Therefore, I will continue to share how to stand solid and focused; trading in the completion spirit instead of this competition driving economy.

Let us take a closer look at the implication of the power of developing a completion motivated spirit.

#COMPLETE

I chose the letter "L" to create a consistent presentation of thoughts surrounding the attitude of completion that kingdom businesspeople expect will make a positive difference as they answer the call for the marketplace.

Letter "L" differentiates these two words, complete and compete. In order to thrive in your assignment in the marketplace, it is necessary that you include this BIG "L."

\# It is a game-changer. We shall expound on this BIG "L" in the following chapters.

The "L" in the word "complete" replaces the toxic feeling of trying to get ahead with the beautiful feeling of purpose.

\# A sense of worth living for because completion means adding to or finishing what someone else started, regarding God's redemptive plan. We are fulfilling the works of God. You are taking your part of being part of the solution of humanity.

The second entry of the meaning of complete in the webster. Complete has several implications as defined by webster dictionary, as "having all necessary parts" "not lacking anything." Another is "not limited in any way".

\#

OTHER MEANINGS TO COMPLETE

1. Finish making or doing.
2. Provide the item or items necessary to make (something) full or entire.

Imagine seeing your trade or business as having all the necessary parts other companies need to improve their service, or how would you feel when you know that you lack nothing because you have it to give knowledgeable service? How will you conduct your enterprise?

"This is what completion is all about. You will eliminate the fear to stand out."

This is what Christ came to do. He came to fulfil or make complete what was writing about Him. Christ was not in competition with anyone. His freedom is unparalleled. Hear one among many of His statements, "I came that they may have life and that more abundantly." This is the language of completion. I read somewhere where an author suggested that the world will be a better place if "L" is added to compete.

Too often, when people engage in business, there is a strong tendency to compete with other fellow businesses.

"His gift of entrepreneurship in you
is a deposit to bring to completion
His love project for the world."

#COMPLETE PRINCIPLE

The marketplace is where the ministry of Jesus finds the most extraordinary expression to complete the work Jesus started. The charge "go into all the world and preach the gospel" by Jesus is directed mainly for the marketplace. The Christian church can bring the transformation Jesus called for, recorded in Matthew 5:13-14.

To complete the restoration God desires, He has anointed marketplace ministers. To bring the full knowledge of Christ into the world by how they will operate in a more sophisticated set of ethical and moral rules. In so doing, they will produce far more results, financially, economically, socially, and emotionally, than any other world principle out there.

"Being the Salt and Light."

Do not ever wonder and struggle anymore with God's ministry to go into all systems to bring it to work the way God intended. It is His purpose! Rather than becoming spiritual critics, we have received the ministry of reconciliation, spiritually, judicially, and commercially.

"To bring completion into the realm of the marketplace."

Market place (People, Planet, Profit)

#

So, far beyond the importance of the marketplace for creating wealth and growing your influence and affluence, the marketplace is also primarily God's ideal space or platform from which He can express His Love for people and the planet.

Remember my start text: John 3:16 and recall the object of his Love is "the World."

God intended to restore the systems for the prosperity of all humanity. Having defined the world as cosmos, the complex organization, and the unseen systems and laws that make the earth function in proper order, we get another insight into what the marketplace represents to God.

Therefore, in direct terms, His gift of entrepreneurship in you is a deposit to bring to completion His love project for the world; meaning that every time an individual answers the call to engage with their assignment in the marketplace, God prospers them. Firstly, due to obedience but subsequently because of the channels that their business will create such that God uses it to express His Love for the world.

This Love is what Paul the Apostle calls the more excellent way, when he concluded the last verse of chapter 12:31…

"But covet earnestly the best gifts: and yet shew I unto you a more excellent way."

All business strives for all-around excellence, whether in the kingdom or not. Desiring this excellent strategy for profitable growth in your business is God's plan for success.

> 1 Corinthians 12:31… But covet earnestly the best gifts: and yet shew I unto you a more excellent way, suggest the secret for excellence in business.

Then following this chapter, he wrote the powerful chapter on Love.

1 Corinthians 13:1-3...If I could speak all the languages of earth and of angels, but didn't love others, I would only be a noisy gong or a clanging cymbal. 2 If I had the gift of prophecy, and if I understood all of God's secret plans and possessed all knowledge, and if I had such faith that I could move mountains, but didn't love others, I would be nothing. 3 If I gave everything I have to the poor and even sacrificed my body, I could boast about it; but if I didn't love others, I would have gained nothing.

#

In the following chapter, Apostle Paul unpacked this excellent way and elaborated it as Love, and I am presenting it as God's referred way for successful entrepreneurship when we decide to employ Love as our way of doing business.

The "L," which is used in this book stands for His Love; God expects you to bring into commerce, stand tall in the middle of the word "compete."

It is God's divine strategy for takeover in the marketplace because, let's face it, if we practice this way excellently as entrepreneurs, we will undoubtedly deliver more remarkable results. Apostle Paul reveals that the most excellent way to be is the way of Love. That is why I chose to show in this book three "L" words as a strategy of God for you to walk on a higher level than how the world expects to succeed.

These "L" words are:

\# Longevity - This is how you need to position your thinking.

\# Lending - This is how you need to align your gifts and Talents.

Loaning - This is how your resource requires to function.

> "Therefore, operating from the space of Love equips us with overcoming skills needed as kingdom entrepreneurship to function above the temptation of competition."

By doing business this way, you will be free from traps of the dark web of stress, lies, and cover-ups. It sets you up with a unique attitude for the marketplace; where your partners and clients will be constantly refreshed and helped by your keen interest for them and your Love for transparency and ethically practices.

And the good news is that everyone customer wants an honest transaction out of the spirit of loyalty and integrity. Therefore, when you familiarize your operations in this new way of thinking and behaviors of the kingdom, which is to operate from the motive of Love, it delivers to you not only the constant flow of inspiration, but it also does the same for your partners and your clientele. (Luke 5:6-7)

Most people will not understand the Love of God until there is an experience of Love; Jesus said some would not believe until they see. However, that's not to say that He is against seeing before believing; on the contrary. Especially in the marketplace, God wants to use His children to demonstrate completion on a whole new level. Firstly let us bring some light on gift activation.

#ACCEPTING AND CULTIVATING GIFT

James 1:17…Every good gift and every perfect gift is from above, and cometh down from the Father of lights, with whom is no variableness, neither shadow of turning.

"Every good and perfect gift is from above," particularly explains that if any person on the planet does not appreciate their gifts and talents, it should not be so for a child of God. The child of God must bring that gift to God as their form of worship.

The word "gift" in this text is from the Greek translation of the word "dorema" which describes a beneficiary of some bountiful treasure/gift.

\# Firstly, God tells of both your spiritual and natural abilities. It is the fact that you can take more risk than others, as it were, or the courage to take more chances for wealth creation; receiving a special gift dealt out from heaven. The spirit of entrepreneurship and the gifts that help and make for successful entrepreneurship is God's indication of His improvement plan for humanity.

\# Secondly, it assures us that in delivering such a special gift to the recipient, He did so with perfect foreknowledge about who you are, "with whom is no variableness, neither shadow of turning," meaning that God is not in doubt about what He gave you as His man or woman representing Him in the marketplace. He is aware of the wealth of contribution you can bring or birth into the earth when you finally accept your God-given gifts and talents.

So, you can only cultivate what you have accepted as intrinsically yours.

#

Imagine if you live on farmland as a renter; even though the land possesses the potential to yield a bumper harvest, you may not have enough motivation to explore all the land has to offer. Likewise, when it comes to your gift, cultivating who you have become from accepting your dreams for enterprises all refer to how your personality is designed, your insight in matters, your taste and inclination in life that brings profit in whatever you set your hands to do. (Deuteronomy 30:9)

"God is saying it is His gift for your life."

#LOVE RELEASE

Corinthians 13: 3…If I gave everything I have to the poor and even sacrificed my body, I could boast about it; but if I didn't love others; I would have gained nothing.

The entire chapter is worth meditating on as a marketplace minister. It is expedient to read and study to discover the power of operating in Love in the marketplace. But in this case, let us consider verse three, for it draws us to the place of one of the essences of doing business the God way. "If I gave everything I have to the poor": In this short phrase, we open up to consider the primary motivation for doing business and suggest for the believer to consider the means and the end in doing business sincerely.

Some may want to argue that the end justifies the means. How? They may say "it doesn't matter how I make money, as long as I give back to my community." God should have no worries with me!

We are reminded to reconsider our passion for success from this text. To be motivated by Love is the power behind getting eternally worthy results. Not only its eternity worthy results, but the scripture goes a long way to equip the believer that operating in Love in the marketplace deals with both your outside and inwards fight with the spirit of competition. Indeed, the marketplace is for giving the and receivership of values.

However, the Spirit of God wants all to prosper in the process. Therefore, any gift that operates from any other motivation other than Love is useless to the Kingdom of God.

Let's expound the scripture a bit, if "I gave everything I have to feed the poor." So, before the acts of charity, the believer must:

\# Firstly, draw all strength from the Love of God which has been imparted by the Holy Spirit at the new birth. (Romans 5:5)

\# Secondly, following the discovery of the unique gift to create wealth for him in the marketplace. (Exodus 31:3 / Deuteronomy 8:18)

God can only establish His kingdom and will on the earth by Love.

\# Thirdly, the difference here in operating in Love in the marketplace may be a foreign concept to the non-Christians, but for the Christian, they have received the supernatural to function at ease on every level. So let Love stand against the pressure of being different, even if others in the marketplace may misplace your intentions at some point. They would soon catch up with your intentions with regard to adding value and completing their needs.

> Romans 5:5…And hope does not put us to shame, because God's Love has been poured out into our hearts through the Holy Spirit, who has been given to us.

The marketplace is God's ultimate tool to impact and influence culture through the gifts He has given to the believer. The best resistance to succeed in a competitive, driven economy is when you choose to operate your business from the place and the power of Love.

The Love factor helps the believer align with the true definition of completion, which is to bring perfection or excellence into the world. (John 3:16 / Mark 16:15)

#LONGEVITY – (TERM THINKING)

*J*ohn 17:3…And this is life eternal, that they might know thee the only true God, and Jesus Christ, whom thou hast sent.

One of the most powerful positions Christ made available to the believer is access to eternity. Thus, we are not waiting to enter into entering; we can and are experiencing eternity right now. Unsurprisingly, this is the reason why many who believe still have the issue of temporal thinking.

Every gift he endows us with does not just have an earthly span, but God designs all his gifts to impact eternity! What a powerful motivation to have as you enter into business. Your business has an eternal impact!

"Your business has an eternal impact!"

Satan's life stops here; it is temporal, and that is why the Bible points out that he is in haste to deceive and cause the world to implode in corruption because he knows that his time is short. (1Peter 5:8)

Hence, it pleases the enemy to drive kingdom business to have the same haste thinking and be tempted with shortcuts and schemes to get rich quickly. Stand against such a primitive mindset!

Decide to walk in the spirit of rest and completion; you have eternity to enjoy the works of your hands! This mindset is rich and essential, yes!

On the one hand, we must be diligent and not become sloppy and lazy, wasting all the time in the world to get our kingdom businesses to become affluent. But we also need to set our eye on eternity so that we do not become hasty or worried at every slight change in the economy.

You have already won the battle of time. Your eternal life guarantees this. The Christian business needs to be the most stable because your budget is not just for five years, but you can see eternity, and your duty to complete God's love project becomes reachable and better supplied with eternity in mind.

#

In other words, God has invited the believer to a world of long-term mindset people. We are structured in the spirit to see things out, and not this get-rich-quick mentality; a path that has led so many into unfortunate fate and financial accidents. Long-term thinking is the path where God challenges us to perpetuate His completion project. It exposes how God thinks about true wealth creation, and how he wants to sustain your relevance in the marketplace.

> Proverb 13:11…Wealth gained hast-
> ily will dwindle, but whoever gathers
> little by little will increase it.

Wealth gain in haste brings to mind a lack of long-term thinking, and it also lacks strategies that can stand the pressure of waiting and faithfulness. Let's look below at faithfulness and how it enables long-term thinking.

#THE SPIRIT OF FAITHFULNESS

Psalms 28:20…A faithful man shall abound with blessings: but he that maketh haste to be rich shall not be innocent.

The faithful means the dedicated and the trustworthy individual who carries out an assignment successfully. The dictionary also defines faithful as being loyal and steadfast. The above scripture identifies that the blessing responds to loyalty, dedication, steadfastness, and trustworthiness.

So, these are words that suggest long-term thinking, planning, and strategies, and the bible text confirms God's favour will be on those who engage with such in mind.

I must introduce the thought that your faith does not ward off the enemy as many people may claim. The reasoning is that faith is insufficient to carry out God's completion project. But it is when you engage in faithful service that breaks the back of poverty and financial failure.

The faithful man will abound with the blessings. Faithfulness is the courage to remain consistent in your chosen discipline. Faithfulness is maintaining a positive attitude toward your God-given vision no matter the fluctuating circumstances in the marketplace.

One who decides to hold their faithful stance in order to maintain Godly standards in their business is the enemy's worst nightmare. Therefore, the Bible says this individual will abound. Abound means to grow and increase in quality, strength, and influence. Abound carries the revelation of a creeper or climbing plant that knows no boundaries but given some time, it will cover the wall over and go over it.

\# That is what was said about Joseph when his aged Father, Jacob, laid his hand to bless him. He blessed him and said, "Joseph is a fruitful bough, even a fruitful bough by a wall; whose branches run over the wall." As you take your stance faithfully in your marketplace assignment, God will continue to supply all the strategies needed to scale up your business.

This supply is called "the blessings." And the blessing declares the endowments with the grace of God to prosper in the will of God.

There is a powerful reference in the book of Philippians, where Apostle Paul points to the fact that he can do all things through Christ, which strengthens Him. (Philippians 4:13…I can do all things through Christ which strengtheneth me)

In essence, he is referring to the principle abound with the blessings; where God supplies His favour, wisdom, and power over your business. He makes it possible for you to outperform in the area you could not break through.

One day, I referenced this text in a friendly conversation, and a well-meaning colleague challenged the notion that if this is true, I can become the prime minister of England. Then he will believe my reasoning for using that text. Well, I quickly interjected that if it is God's will for my life, then surely, He will endow me with all I need to get there. This text is not generalizing God's power to supply, but it confirms the fact that when you submit to the will of God for your life, then in that marketplace where He positions you to establish His purpose on the earth, you can do all things through Christ (the anointing) which strengthens you.

Therefore, it is essential that you align your heart to walk in your business with His grace faithfully. Most of the challenges and possible delays you may encounter in the marketplace will be around faithfulness and how you carry God's Love entrusted to you to complete His Love as you advance into the future.

"Let us consider the story of Martha and Mary as we explore faithfulness in light of the marketplace."

#MARY AND MARTHA PRINCIPLE

It is crucial for your kingdom completion project to think about long-term or to take the mind place seriously. It is so easy to drift away in your daily challenges and business chores if I may call it that. I am in no way, shape, or form trivializing what goes on in the day to day running of your business, such as meeting deadlines, meetings with staff, dealing with suppliers, the list goes on.

However, this mind place for a kingdom entrepreneur in the spirit is powerful. You want to maintain a certain quality of rest and avoid all anxiety. To highlight this fact, I will use the familiar story of Martha and Mary.

Metaphorically, we all deal with the Martha and Mary perspectives respectfully. Because there is a Martha and a Mary wrestle in all those business-people representing God in the marketplace.

Martha describes that place where we get so engaged, busy, and perturbed by the many schedules, but there is a place in you that calls for rest and quality time with the Master; this is the Mary place in you.

What is the key? And how do you manage these places? Let me expand.

Martha was also beneficial to the Lord; otherwise, He would not go to enjoy her (Martha) heart of hospitality, serving the food and drinks and maintaining the atmosphere of Love and friendship. The scripture points to the fact that Jesus Loved them.

The Master relied on and loved her faithfulness and availability. As we read, further in the scripture, we can see that they were Jesus's friends. Clearly, that was not the first time they may have welcomed Jesus. But in this visit, Martha will learn a valuable lesson; and through her experience, we will all receive valuable keys to kingdom expansion.

"The Martha in you is valuable."

Let me paint a picture. Let's say your business has picked up and grown, and you are preparing for the kingdom by your engagement in your assignment. Everything is growing in your influence and affluence, such that the Lord is meeting your needs to impact society: The Martha in you is that mental place that keeps the ball rolling, as it were. As I touched on earlier, to meet all demands, and this, until the load becomes heavy, it is at this point the Mary in you will call to your attention.

The Lord loves the "Martha" in you; she met all Jesus's needs when He passed by with His disciples. There is an excellent reward received because of her faithfulness in the presence of the Master. She "abounded!"

Do not be troubled about your so-called "workaholic" behaviour that others may label you by. Vey often Martha is portrayed in such negative light in bible teaching. For the record, the Master only called her to rest this once. And she did not object to The Master's instruction because she loved him.

#

I am only suggesting that the key is to remember to respond to this call to rest no matter your faithfulness. Satan knows how to keep the "Martha" in you engaged doing the right things in the wrong way until you may feel tired and critical.

As a kingdom businesses person, do not take your eyes off the concept of completion; and trusting the Master to take your time in rest is crucial doing it The Mary way!

> Luke 10:42…But one thing is needful: and Mary hath chosen that good part, which shall not be taken away from her.

Let me expand. The master key that empowers you to engage in the "completion" project is understanding when to rest and collaborating with the Master to complete His assignment effectively.

\# Firstly, Jesus commended Mary that she chose the good part. What was the good part? Rest and collaboration. The "Mary" in you will draw your understanding that you are not working alone. Martha felt she was working alone. You may become resentful because of your work ethics, misunderstood, especially by those who in your opinion are simply "sitting and doing nothing for God," or worse yet, you may move into murmuring. These all-satanic influenced thoughts, you will have to fight off.

\# Secondly, there is a deep sense of loneliness that may accompany businesspeople in the kingdom when faced with the reality of how time, in essence, is not on our side, and the greed, deceit, and hardheartedness in the marketplace may cause lots of temptations to move out of faithfulness into casual stewardship of your kingdom resource.

Therefore, you need to connect radically with the call of the "Mary" in you. Responding to this call to resting is what the "Mary" in you is all about. Jesus loves this place. He calls it the "good part."

A "part" so instrumental to your continued faithfulness and long-term thinking. For times when your assignment, becomes a chore rather than a song or melody. When you are pushing and pulling, where the load becomes heavy, there is a "Mary" in every kingdom entrepreneur that calls for worship, prayer, and reading in order to enjoy a time of refreshing in God's presence.

"You are not alone."

God wants your business to succeed more than you can ever fathom. He has more at stake to help you achieve than anyone can imagine. Success to God spells, He has one more channel in the earth to help and bless others by alleviating suffering and bringing hope. The World is His responsibility, and by blessing you with gifts, talents, and favour, He reaches the needs of humanity.

It is imperative that you cut out and spend large chunks of your time at the feet of Jesus. Many may believe that if I spend time with the Master, what time do I have to run my business? Knowing my schedules and deadlines may fall apart, I cannot sit idle that long. Your business is not yours; it is the Lords. Think collaboration!

\# Collaboration means "to co- labour." Jesus is a vital labourer in any vision he gives. He is not a silent partner, nor is he an angel investor; he is the owner of your business. That is why the union of "Mary" to him is one of receiving vital plans and strategies for the future of your business. Notice Jesus affirms the fact that Mary was drawing valuable insight from Him, which will solidify her place in his (The Lord's) Kingdom completion project.

It will be great for you to establish a day where you answer the call of the "Mary" in you. As you engage in prolonged times of prayer, fasting and meditating on your assignments as kingdom entrepreneurs, this is a space that will defeat the feeling of competition in you. It is the space where you create large room in courage for rest and a developed revelation of divine collaboration for a long-lasting impact.

#LENDING YOUR SERVICE

onitoring place (Establishing the Kingdom of God)

Ephesians 6:6-7...Not with eyeservice, as men-pleasers; but as the servants of Christ, doing the will of God from the heart; 7 With good will doing service, as to the Lord, and not to men:

The end goal of your business is rated higher than any of our earthly pleasures. In our world today, every stimulus is geared to pleasure and self-gratification, and indulgence in the fine things of life. So, living and doing business to complete the Kingdom of God on earth is such a priceless mindset to harness in your business.

One of the consequences of the spirit of competition is the delay to influence and the havoc it wreaks in many kingdom businesspeople in the process. The schools of business have imprinted particular adverse concepts of doing business.

That is so counter kingdom culture: For example, "take ownreship of your talent and gifting, becoming a self-made entrepreneur," even down to the place of saving large sums for retirement. Now all these are great disciplines, and really, it is not easy to have such focus let alone to achieve them.

The flip side is that once we allow these acquired thoughts to become entrenched in our business language as kingdom entrepreneurs, we will enable the enemy to control and corrupts how we render and receive service. The enemy turns the believer inward to compete for even the idea of releasing resources for kingdom expansion.

The purpose of all enterprises is wealth creation and wealth distribution. Completion is the base principle that facilitates creation and distribution processes.

"With goodwill doing service, as
to the Lord, and not to men."

\# Goodwill doing service is such a powerful motivation to adapt when you want to be ahead in completing your assignment. Inspired by God is the understanding that all we have, has been lent from the Master.

Lending is the activity of lending people and organisations resources which they pay back in interest. How does this fit in the program of completion?

Let's look at this in the confines, where a start-up business completes their business research, fine-tune their mission and vision statements, finished market research and analysis, product analysis, client listing, and all they need to have an excellent beginning.

However, one of the crucial points in their step is fundraising, without which many start-ups have been frustrated, but let's say our start-up lands a significant sponsor; this sponsor is helping our start-up complete its business dreams.

#

Drawing from the above discussion, in the Kingdom, God is the great lender of all resources, whether in the form of finances, special talent and giftings, great concepts and ideas, and the burst of creativity. They are all forms of lending heaven gives to its businesspeople venturing out to expand the influence and affluence of His kingdom in the earth.

James 1:17...Every good and perfect gift is from above, coming down from the Father of the heavenly lights, who does not change like shifting shadows. (NIV)

For me, the keyword here is "every"; making these power gifts that potentially have the power to change the world, as a thing that God possesses and is in control of and is willing to give to anyone ready to act on His behalf.

Here is how Apostle Paul reveals it in 1Corinthians 12:11...All these [gifts, achievements, abilities] are inspired and brought to pass by one, and the same [Holy] Spirit, who apportions to each person individually [exactly] as He chooses. (AMP)

\# I love this part: "Who apportions to each person individually [exactly] as He chooses." In other words, the Master was deliberate in apportioning gifts and callings perfectly to individuals to fulfil His desire in His completion project.

Let's look back at our start-up again. It is safe to assume that after the financial help, our businessperson will only become more sensitive to the daily running of the business. The lender's voice will take on more sway in their decision-making processes than any other voice. I will be bold to say our start-up business will be willing to ignore the voice of the market for the opinion of his new-found lender. With such strong and bold perspectives, I am portraying how being introduced to the lending place in God's "Completion project" is so important. We feel that we are solely responsible for pleasing the Father through our enterprise because he is the lender.

Of course, there is a spiritual danger when we do not see the Master as Lender; an entitlement spirit sprouts up in the heart surrounding the issues of distributing the profits and influence that the business has attained.

The bible passage below will shed some more light on this!

> Luke 12:16…And he spake a parable unto them, saying, "The ground of a certain rich man brought forth plentifully: 17…And he thought within himself saying, what shall I do, because I have no room where to bestow my fruits?" And he said, this will I do: I will pull down my barns and build greater; and there will I bestow all my fruits and my goods. And I will say to my soul, Soul, thou hast much goods laid up for many years; take thine ease, eat, drink, and be merry. But God said unto him, Thou fool, this night thy

soul shall be required of thee: then whose shall those things be, which thou hast provided? So is he that layeth up treasure for himself and is not rich toward God. (KJV)

This gentleman in the above-mentioned text, missed the Lending place of kingdom establishment. Let's define the sub-topic of this chapter, "monitoring" from Wikipedia's notes on monitoring NGO projects. It states Monitoring and Evaluation (M&E) is used to assess the performance of tasks, institutions, and programs set up by governments, international organisations, and NGOs. Its goal is to improve current and future management of outputs, outcomes, and impact.

We can deduce even from this definition that God takes His businesspeople through a series of monitoring and evaluation processes. And how they mature as He takes His businesspeople through lending, growing, and multiplication processes.

He monitors your progress with the intent that you are not tempted into lust with entitlement.

"He takes account with you because we alluded that He is an active owner and not a partner."

\#

The subject in our text started well and became a very successful businessman. The story goes, because his ground produced for him, this is a type of God's favour. Because of the blessing on his land, his crop multiplied much that he landed with a bumper harvest. But he was more interested in hoarding and self-gratification. he says,

\# I will pull down my barns and build greater; and there will I bestow all my fruits and my goods.

\# Competition breaks down what was helpful in first instance to show that it can do better. That is the sad news about the competition. You see this overtly in developing economies, where the economy is always in a jumpstart mode due to this spirit of competition. Every leader who takes the helm of power breaks down a system to build a new and better system, which never gets off the ground because before they start, another comes in and breaks it down. And the vicious circle begins all over.

The purpose he stated for breaking the first system of wealth creation was not because he saw the need to add value to God's completion plan but to enjoy more and more significant success for himself. He created substantial wealth but missed the end goal of the Master's wealth distribution program. Such as by financing godly projects, or community development. It is interesting how many business people have the internal struggles to compete daily with their own success at times and lose their eternal purpose.

"So is he that layeth up treasure for himself and is not rich toward God."

"Considering your understanding that he lends you to profit the kingdom and become rich toward God. You will enter into the secret of the continual flow of resources from God while you experience defense against the devourer."

\#

Notice the goal is to improve income, output, outcome, and impact. Hence, the lending place (monitoring place) is where God separated his businesses for higher promotion and more significant influence.

\# When the kingdom entrepreneur adopts the concept of completion, lending, and the understanding to make available your possession for more substantial impact for the kingdom; your struggle for favour will be over.

To become a vital candidate to carry out God's completion project, you need this servant attitude where your goal is serving with your talent, gift, and idea as a payback to God's lending system. To that businessperson, it takes us out of the competition of day-to-day hassle to the peace of completing God's agenda for the earth with joy.

\# The lender (God) did not help you start competing; instead, He established you to fulfil what needed fulfilment. Jesus said this (in my own words) "I did not come to compete with Moses or Elijah, I came to complete what I started through their life and ministry." (Matthew 5:17)

Likewise, as you think and meditate on the Lending place, you will slowly realize where God wants to complete in His great plan through your business.

#LOANED

"God's Wealth distribution plan."

This last chapter will highlight the struggles that many feel when it comes to entirely relying on God to exercise their dominion over the forces that prevent the righteous from fully expressing the grace of God in their business.

Firstly, let us deal with the reason why God promotes your business. It may interest you that His motive is a long-standing covenant of completion

He made with Abraham, who we now refer to as the Father of Faith. Read the below text.

Deuteronomy 8:18…Thou shalt remember the Lord thy God: for it is he that giveth thee power to get wealth, that he may establish his covenant which he sware unto thy fathers, as it is this day. (KJV)

In this scripture, God highlighted the reasons He sends prosperity. The primary reason is that He wants to forward his completion plan covenanted with His friend Abraham concerning the whole world. (Genesis 12:1-3)

In the book of Romans, Apostle Paul made it clear how extensive this plan with Abraham is. Essentially, that plan is to Govern and take back the whole earth and re-establish it as God's garden of righteousness, peace, and Joy. Read what Paul said about this Covenant.

> Romans 4:13…For the promise, that he should be the heir of the world, was not to Abraham, or his seed, through the law, but through the righteousness of faith.

God does not just reign over religious affairs. In my most used phrase, in which I state that "God is not a Christian; He is a King," I draw the listener's attention. God cannot be locked down only in the confines of religion, but his rule is the affairs of humanity.

\# He is a King means: He is not only responsible to meet the needs of the Christian, but He is also responsible to provide for all people and His creation. He incentivizes the businesspeople to examine this spiritual reality. (Matthew 5:43-48)

Notice that every significant event God used as the agency for change in history was not a religious change. It is often the environment in the case of Noah and his family, in the case of Sodom and Gomorrah was morality and ethics; it was a humanitarian issue in the case of Egypt and the enslaving humanity. In Babylon, it was that case of tyranny and power. The point is that He is God.

When I say loan, I am speaking as an entrepreneur. It is very important that you quickly realize that God will loan you everything you need as long as you will enforce His Love in the earth as He desires. That your attention will be that of excellent stewardship. (Proverbs 10:22)

#

Below is a background to why God destroyed the civilization that occupied the promised land to loan it to the children of Israel.

> Deuteronomy 9: 1...Hear, O Israel: Thou art to pass over Jordan this day, to go in to possess nations greater and mightier than thyself, cities great and fenced up to heaven,2 A people great

and tall, the children of the Anakims, whom thou knowest, and of whom thou hast heard say, who can stand before the children of Anak!

3 Understand therefore this day, that the Lord thy God is he which goeth over before thee; as a consuming fire he shall destroy them, and he shall bring them down before thy face: so shalt thou drive them out, and destroy them quickly, as the Lord hath said unto thee.

4 Speak not thou in thine heart, after that the Lord thy God hath cast them out from before thee, saying, for my righteousness the Lord hath brought me in to possess this land: but for the wickedness of these nations the Lord doth drive them out from before thee.

"I Understand that many may have this conflict because the action does not attest to the character of a loving God."

It is essential to grasp that God has a purpose for every piece of real estate as the owner of every land on the earth. It is His responsibility to see that this divine purpose for each real estate is not hindered by the behaviour of the occupant of the land. (Psalms 24:1)

These Canaanites made up the group of inhabitants when God was ready to bring in His new occupiers; God had allowed the Canaanites the space of four hundred years to bring prosperity and excellent stewardship. He allowed enough time for this nation to bring fruit for the next generation.

They were the cause of continued degradation of the soul and life on the earth.

#

The Canaanites destroyed the next generation with the fertility cults (killing the unborn) and their firstborns in sacrifice, sexual Immorality and pagan worship. These were expensive lifestyles that proved unsustainable in ancient economies, also in modern times, to say the least. As a consequence, God called them wicked and not suitable to continue to waste His resource.

God promised Abraham that if he walked before Him and be perfect (wholehearted and mature), He would make Abraham the custodian of all the affairs of humanity. Abraham believed in God's reward system and bought into the idea that God, through him (Abraham) God will teach the world how to break the power of poverty and stop human suffering through him. (Abraham)

When He shows us how to live and do business with each other. It provokes heaven to bring forth the privilege. Now, God can have access at all levels in life to bless humanity. God's desire is for the world to be instructed and governed by faith in God and the principles kingdom of God.

There is a tendency when people are in business to immediately assume they are in business to have their needs met. Well, indeed, that is worth the consideration. It is good business to do your due diligence to ensure that the figures match up and all outgoing and incoming are in sync.

God wants to meet all your needs; and thereafter, He can continue to create opportunities for your overflow so that you can become God's arm to fulfil His need to serve others.

\# As a kingdom entrepreneur, the world is your marketplace. God has destined your business to be a global entity; to become a source of blessing and prosperity.

\#

His plan is for your enterprise to nourish the world with all the beauties from heaven. Your business is a symbol of His gift to humanity. God gave you gifts and talents on loan to join His massive army of gifted individuals to help engineer his promise to manifestation. (In Genesis 12:1-3, you can read the full extent of God desire and plans for the world)

Matthew 6:24… "No man can serve two masters: for either he will hate the one and love the other; or else he will hold to the one, and despise the other. Ye cannot serve God and mammon."

Although I have done an extensive study on mammon, I can only allude to the lure people's businesses may have toward wanting to hoard what the Lord is investing in them.

\# Mammon is not money or the power behind the use of money, but mammon is the Canaanite God that instigates greed and reverence for the material world. It demands that individuals perpetuate wicked worship, as mentioned earlier. Mammon ridicules the worship of God with your substance; he is the author who feeds fear and the poverty syndrome that make individuals chase after money and the uncertain luxuries it promises to bring. Mammon is the god behind the drive to work hard but spend hard at the altar of sex, drug, fame, and eventually the death of morals and ethics.

> Deuteronomy 12:1...These are the statutes and judgments, which ye shall observe to do in the land, which the Lord God of thy fathers giveth thee to possess it, all the days that ye live upon the earth.

> 2 Ye shall utterly destroy all the places, wherein the nations which ye shall possess served their gods, upon the high mountains, and upon the hills, and under every green tree:

3 And ye shall overthrow their altars, and break their pillars, and burn their groves with fire; and ye shall hew down the graven images of their gods and destroy the names of them out of that place.

4 Ye shall not do so unto the Lord your God.

5 But unto the place which the Lord your God shall choose out of all your tribes to put his name there, even unto his habitation shall ye seek, and thither thou shalt come

\# The world system encourages and endorses doing business by honing skills like cheating, manipulation, and hoarding for gain. These are part of the influence of mammon. They accumulate relevant information from public view, and they do so with financial resources, natural resources, and human resources, which creates hardship and the failing economies we see around the world now.

The above-stated are the ways the media are propagating you do business, but the systems that drive this hunger cannot stand the test of the Lord.

\# In the text we read, this way of doing business was so inferior to the kingdom system that after four hundred years in the ownership of the Canaanites, God still commanded that his people tear down everything they built. Their strategy, design, and lifestyle were worthless under divine scrutiny.

I like the warnings of the Lord to His people… "Ye shall not do so unto the Lord your God." This means when your time comes, build differently; build with excellence! So, "take your loan from me more seriously," God says, and become a better steward of what He loaned you.

"The last piece I want to discuss is adapting the humble spirit in God's divine loaning system to complete his redemptive plan on the earth."

No doubt, it will take a vast amount of financial resources to engage your assignment and complete it. Because as you go for completion, the enemy will do all he can to distract you in all kinds of ways, financially, fraudulent people, false believers, wrong covenants partner, you name it, but do not become competitive!

\# Always keep your grace on you. God has more than a million ways to respond to all who tampers with His resources.

So, the perspective of loaning from God is a crucial topic; if you will excel in the business world where competition is the standard operating system; seeing the big picture that all we have is a loaned from God and with the deep intention for wealth distribution. This is all your advantage, and you will function well above your natural capacity because His favour will be added to you.

Think Loaning from God!

When you want to get involved in God's wealth distribution plan and to finance His projects in the nations. Speak of God's wealth distribution strategies; if there are any delays to access true wealth, it may be the budding reality or the unawareness that we loan from God.

"If you will allow my re-emphasis, that these loans include our talents, developed skills, special endowment, creative visions, and natural and spiritual gifts."

#SURRENDER

When believers surrender to this revelation, God will pour out His blessings for a more significant impact of His kingdom in your life and business. I see loaning from God as a spiritual birthing place of grand dreams and vision.

"So, gifts came from above as loans for human flourishing for all intent and purpose."

Hence completion deals with the competition of pulling down one another. Instead, as kingdom entrepreneurs, money is a stream that needs to keep flowing from one to another, enriching one another. Finances and property distribution have always been the elephant in the room for church people.

Many know how important it is to expand the kingdom of God, but few are determined to address it and take their place in wealth creation. I trust you are one if you have read this far. God has a unique plan to make you rich beyond your wildest dreams.

> "When we discover the concept of loaning from God in business, no one needs to pull another down."

In the previous chapter, the man in the parable resolves to pull down his achievement because he wants to hoard more than is necessary. This is a sign of a perpetual cycle of competition with one former achievement, and the drive to remove structures that are already standing has been the downfall for many well-meaning individuals.

As a believer in Christ, you will be tempted to act and have the same competitive spirit. You will have to walk in a way whereby the difference will be clear. The scripture text above calls this man a fool because his heart was set in "competition mode" with prosperity.

He plans to prevent the flow of God's blessings and truncate God's plan for wealth distribution for his community. In the world, this will be termed good management, but in the Kingdom, it is foolishness.

Because he may have started a project about how to help other farmers improve on their nursery or planting processes for maximum results. By doing so, he spreads prosperity to a greater extent in the region or shares his knowledge on a more influential platform for added significant impact on lives. Also, to give out his excess produce because he was comfortable in the first place. But he lost sight of the principle of God's wealth distribution for the prosperity of all.

His indictment was that he was "not rich toward God," which means he compromised his opportunity to become significant in God's completion project for the planet.

It is my pleasure to present you with these three mind mines, that when they explode in you, your Kingdom influence and affluence will move nations to the saving grace of God!

About the Author

He is a dynamic teacher, Pastor, author, speaker, leadership consultant, facilitator, and business trainer. He is the founder and Senior Pastor of Claypot Church International. A ministry committed to raising leaders and impacting lives around the world. He founded the Tulip Seminars, which is a division of Tulip publication.

Tulip seminar aims to bring seasoned masterminds and leadership to facilitate leaders with values and strategies that empowers private and public performance for growth in ministry, business, and leadership.

He is married to Judith Emoghene who co-Pastors with him and A qualified Natural health minister with Hallelujah Acres. Currently, she is leading her health centre and recreation project for healing the body with natural foods.

He has authored a number of books including: - Sounds Of The Last Days, Get In Line With Your Destiny, I Will Build, Love In Action, Know Yourself, Overcomers Life.